W9-AUY-482

ALONG the LUANGWA

A Story of an African Floodplain

by Schuyler Bull

Illustrated by Alan Male

Soundprints
Where Children Discover...

To the Talbots, for encouraging me to take the plunge,
and to my parents for understanding when I did — S.B.

To my daughters Sophie and Chloe — A.M.

Book copyright © 1999 Futech Interactive Products, Inc., Phoenix, AZ 85018.

Published by Soundprints, an imprint of Futech Interactive Products, Inc.,
353 Main Avenue, Norwalk, Connecticut 06851.

Book layout: Diane Hinze Kanzler
Editor: Judy Gitenstein

First Edition 1999
10 9 8 7 6 5 4 3 2 1
Printed in Hong Kong

Acknowledgments:
Our thanks to Michael Devlin of the Endangered Wildlife Trust for his curatorial review.

Library of Congress Cataloging-in-Publication Data

Bull, Schuyler.
    Along the Luangwa: a story of an African floodplain / written by Schuyler Bull;
illustrated by Alan Male. — 1st ed.
        p.   cm.
    Summary: Explores life in Zambia's Luangwa River Valley as seen through the eyes
of a mother crocodile and her newly hatched babies.
    ISBN 1-56899-776-0 (hardcover)   ISBN 1-56899-777-9 (pbk.)
    1. Nile crocodile — Luangwa River Valley (Zambia and Mozambique) Juvenile
literature. [1. Crocodiles.   2. Ecology — Luangwa River Valley (Zambia and
Mozambique)]   I. Male, Alan, ill.   II. Title.
    QL666.C925B85   1999
    597.98 — dc21   99-25917
                                                                                                  CIP
                                                                                                  AC

ALONG the LUANGWA

A Story of an African Floodplain

by Schuyler Bull

Illustrated by Alan Male

The
Nature
Conservancy®

The crescent moon hovers over the horizon, casting its silver light on the Luangwa River Valley. Bats dart through the trees, hunting for insects. In the safety of the tall grasses, a small herd of kudus doze. A few miles from the banks of the river, a mother crocodile lies waiting in the sandy soil. She has faithfully protected her nest all winter. Tonight her wait is over.

Squeak. Chirp. *Crack*. The babies are hatching! Their squawks and chirps come from under the sandy soil of the nest.

With her massive claws, the mother crocodile paws at the earth until she sees a small tail, then another, and little heads. By the time the horizon turns a shimmering pink, nearly fifty baby crocodiles wriggle and squirm in the pit.

The mother gently scoops up fifteen babies
in her mouth and carries them to a small pool
nearby. She makes several trips back and forth
until her whole brood is safe. But she must move
swiftly. The noise and smell of the hatchlings
will soon attract marabous, monitor lizards,
and other predators.

The young crocs slide into the pool nose first.
A soft-shelled turtle swims by, startled from his
warm spot on the edge of the pond.

It is now morning. The newborn crocodiles
watch the golden circle of the sun crest over
the limbs of a tamarind tree, flooding the river
with its light.

A water bug skates across the surface
between floating pieces of water lettuce. Even
at his young age, the newly-hatched crocodile
watches the bug carefully, preparing to pounce
on his first meal.

After his breakfast, the young croc spies a Tilapia bream darting back and forth in the water. He follows the fish to its floating nest of grass and other pieces of water plants. When the croc gets too close, the bream turns and chases him away from the nest.

All afternoon, the crocs float in the pool. They float with just their eyes and nostrils above the water so they can breathe and keep an eye out for predators. Overhead, the sun beats down on them.

9

It is now June, the dry season. It has not rained for many weeks. There are no more tadpoles or water bugs in the nursery pool. The crocodile family must move to the Luangwa River.

They set out just before dawn. The mother crocodile hurries her brood down a path that looks like a grassy tunnel. Suddenly she crashes off the path, her large jaws snapping wildly. The baby crocs scurry for cover.

The mother has found a marabou that has been stalking the babies from the tall grasses nearby. The large bird flies off over the ivory palm. Safe once again, the crocodiles resume their journey.

The sun has already risen by the time they finally reach the river. Other crocodiles line the banks of the river. Some males are over ten feet long! Yellow-billed storks and open-billed storks stand still in large flocks. Hippos wallow in the middle of the river, snorting and blowing water out of their nostrils.

The younger crocodiles pause as their mother eases herself into the water. Across the river, hundreds of carmine bee-eaters dart in and out of their nests in the riverbank to catch insects flying over the water. Others dive into the water for a quick bath.

Far downriver, a tall saddle-billed stork stirs the mud with its feet, hunting for snails and clams. It finds a small fish and tosses it up in the air before catching and swallowing it.

The babies watch their mother cautiously before sliding into the water to begin their search for bugs and small fish. One young croc paddles to the far end of the river where catfish stare up at him from the deep pools. As he nears the deepest area, he hears the call of a fish eagle.

The baby croc cries out a distress signal. He sees the curled sharp talons of the bird as he dives under the water. He hears a splash as the bird follows.

15

The baby crocodile resurfaces and sees the bird once more. In the sharp talons, a catfish wriggles and flops as the eagle flies along the surface of the water. Instantly the mother crocodile appears. She quickly herds him toward shore.

From a safe place among the papyrus, the young crocodile watches the eagle veer up to its nest, lugging the heavy fish along with it.

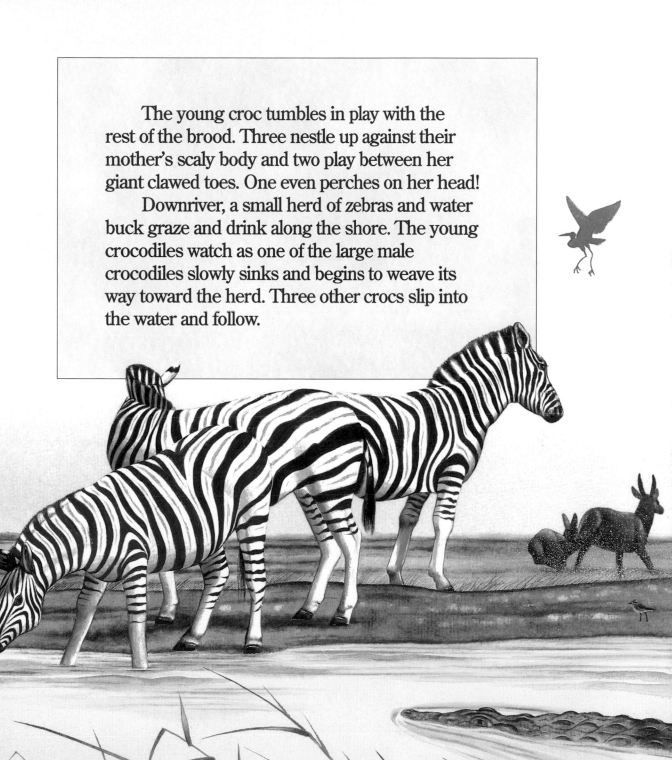

The young croc tumbles in play with the rest of the brood. Three nestle up against their mother's scaly body and two play between her giant clawed toes. One even perches on her head!

Downriver, a small herd of zebras and water buck graze and drink along the shore. The young crocodiles watch as one of the large male crocodiles slowly sinks and begins to weave its way toward the herd. Three other crocs slip into the water and follow.

The crocodiles seem to work as a team as they approach the herd. They are almost nose-to-nosc with the beasts. Suddenly the largest croc leaps from the water, gnashing his jaws. The herd bolts! The crocodiles churn the water with their powerful tails and bodies, but the zebras and water buck are already safe on land.

Still hungry, the crocodiles hunt for fish and snails in the shallower parts of the river. Using their scaly bodies like fishing nets, they herd the fish into the shore. But even the fish are becoming scarce as the drought continues.

Many other animals suffer from the drought. In the morning, the larger crocodiles are more successful in finding food. One crocodile takes a turn holding the animal carcass in its jaws as a second croc spins itself in the water to loosen a more manageable bite. A tall goliath heron stands nearby, watching for scraps.

The crocodiles take turns eating until every one has had something to eat.

In the afternoon, the sun glares down, baking the muddy banks of the river. Huge pools of water are still, unable to cross over the small bridges of mud where the river is more shallow. Even the bee-eaters are still in the midday sun.

The young crocodiles head to the water to escape the heat. The mother croc, her mouth wide open to cool herself, guards them from the muddy shore. A plover darts in and out of her giant mouth, cleaning her teeth.

A few days later, the rain finally comes.
Soon small fish and tadpoles return to the waters.
The pools fill and spill over the muddy bridges,
sending the waters of the Luangwa River
rushing downstream.

At night, the crocodiles pull themselves
high up onto the banks of the river. Animals call
through the brush around the river. It is cool
and clear in the fresh new grasses where the
crocodiles sleep. The silver moon rises above
them and shimmers down over the flowing waters
of the Luangwa River.

27

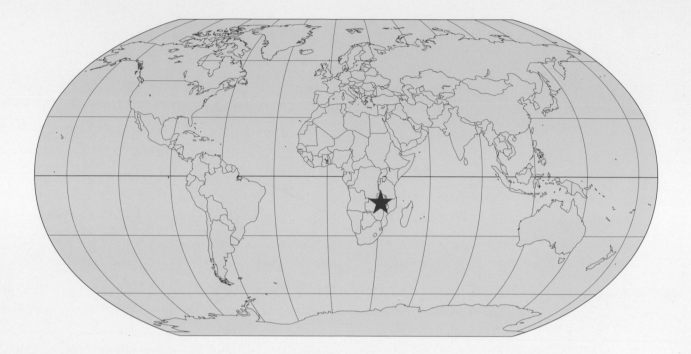

The Luangwa River Valley, Zambia, Africa

The Luangwa River Valley, in eastern Zambia, is one of the best wildlife sanctuaries in the world. Populations of the endangered black rhinos, giraffes, abundant herds of hippopotamuses and elephants, and various species of antelope are the most concentrated in all of Africa. With over four hundred species, the area is also famous for its bird populations.

About an African Floodplain

The Luangwa River Valley is one of the few places where Nile crocodiles still thrive in the wild. Crocodiles are one of the "great survivors" of the animal kingdom. Ancestors of the Nile crocodiles can be traced back to the Great Age of Reptiles over seventy million years ago. They are one of the only creatures to have outlived the dinosaurs.

Some scientists think that crocodiles' longevity is due to their special abilities. Crocodiles have many physical advantages, such as sharp teeth and armor-like skin. Crocodiles also have a special ability to sink or float when they want to.

Crocodiles have other ways of working together to help survive. A crocodile's jaws do not move sideways, so they cannot chew. Instead, they rip off pieces of meat and swallow them—bone, hair, and all. When there is a large enough group of crocodiles, they will act together. The largest male usually starts the feast. One or two crocodiles brace their meal as others tear off smaller bits by spinning themselves in the water. They will not stop until every crocodile has eaten.

There are almost no Nile crocodiles in the actual Nile River today. Damming projects and new cities along the Nile's shores have destroyed or disrupted the crocodile's natural habitat.

Today thousands of tourists visit Zambia to see the variety of plants, birds, and animals which live in the safety of the country's four national parks. Safaris and guided tours allow people to experience these special animals living in their native habitats while causing little harm to the creatures themselves.

Glossary

▲ *Acacia with weaver bird nests*

▲ *Herald or red-lipped snake*

▲ *Nile catfish*

▲ *African fish eagle*

▲ *Kafue lechwe*

▲ *Nile crocodile*

▲ *Common waterbuck*

▲ *Marabou stork*

▲ *Open-billed stork*

▲ *Goliath heron*

▲ *Marsh or helmeted terrapin*

▲ *Papyrus*

▲ *Hammer-headed bat*

▲ *Mouthbrooder or tilapia bream*

▲ *Southern giraffe*

▲ *African elephant*

▲ *Chapman's zebra*

▲ *Sable antelope*

▲ *African hawk eagle*

▲ *Greater kudu*

▲ *Saddle-billed stork*

▲ *Black rhinoceros*

▲ *Hippopotamus*

▲ *Woodland kingfisher*

▲ *Carmine bee-eater*

▲ *Kittlitz's plover*

▲ *Yellow-billed stork*